Contents

Introduction
Easy to underestimate

Solvents are chemicals which are used as ingredients in a variety of products. They are so widespread in everyday life that it's estimated that in the average Western household there are at least 30 products containing solvents. These chemicals are found in glues, cleaning products, aerosols, lighter fuel, paint, and many others, and it would be almost impossible to create a solvent-free environment.

Unfortunately, some of the properties that make solvents useful also give them the potential to be abused. Solvents are 'volatile substances', which means that they are substances that evaporate quickly. They may be gases (when at room temperature) or liquids that give off vapours. Some people deliberately breathe in, or inhale, these gases or vapours to cause intoxication or a 'high'. The products most commonly abused in this way include certain brands of fuel gases, glues and aerosols. The intoxication usually wears off very quickly, but there are many unpleasant side effects.

Why is inhaling solvents dangerous?
The main side effect of solvent abuse that brings the user to the attention of others is death. This is often sudden, due to the heart stopping, suffocation, or trauma such as falls or road accidents. Many of the young people who die from solvent abuse are killed the first time they try inhaling, and there is no way to reduce this risk, apart from never abusing solvents in the first place. Although this may sound an extreme statement, it is supported by a considerable body of evidence, and it's important to be as clear as possible that solvent abuse can and does kill without warning.

Use ...
Modern glues are made from chemicals and are designed to dry quickly and form a strong bond.

SOLVENTS

Karla Fitzhugh

HODDER
Wayland

an imprint of Hodder Children's Books

© 2003 White-Thomson Publishing Ltd

White-Thomson Publishing Ltd,
2-3 St Andrew's Place, Lewes,
East Sussex BN7 1UP

Published in Great Britain in 2003 by Hodder Wayland, an imprint of Hodder Children's Books

This paperback edition published in 2005

This book was produced for White-Thomson Publishing Ltd by Ruth Nason.

Design: Carole Binding
Picture research: Glass Onion Pictures

The right of Karla Fitzhugh to be identified as the author of this work has been asserted by her in accordance with the Copyright, Designs and Patents Act 1988.

British Library Cataloguing in Publication Data
Karla Fitzhugh
  Solvents. - (Health Issues)
  1. Solvents - Health aspects - Juvenile literature 2. Solvent abuse - Juvenile literature
  I. Title
  613.8
ISBN 0 7502 4375 9

Printed in China by WKT Company Limited

Hodder Children's Books
A division of Hodder Headline Limited
338 Euston Road, London NW1 3BH

Acknowledgements

The author and publishers thank the following for their permission to reproduce photographs and illustrations: Carole Binding: page 12; Martyn Chillmaid: page 59; Corbis Images: pages 5 (John Heseltine), 10t (Jim Craigmyle), 12 (Pablo Corral), 27 (John Madere Photography), 44 (Jennie Woodcock, Reflections Photolibrary), 47 (Jose Luis Pelaez, Inc.), 50 (Steve McDonough); Angela Hampton Family Life Picture Library: pages 13, 19, 22, 23, 26, 30, 35, 43, 48, 56, 57; Impact Photos: pages 11 (Giles Barnard), 32 (Mark Cator), 51 (Bruce Stephens); Mediscan: page 33; Science Photo Library: pages 4 (Klaus Guldbrandsen), 6 (Philippe Rocher, Jerrican), 9 (Sinclair Stammers), 15 (John Greim), 20 (Jean-Loup Charmet), 58 (Mauro Fermariello); Topham/ImageWorks: pages 16, 24, 40, 45, 49, 52-53: John Walmsley: page 38. The photographs on the cover, pages 1, 28 and 54 are from the Hodder Wayland Picture Library. The illustrations on pages 8, 10, 18, 36 and 37 are by Carole Binding.

Note: Photographs illustrating the case studies in this book were posed by models.

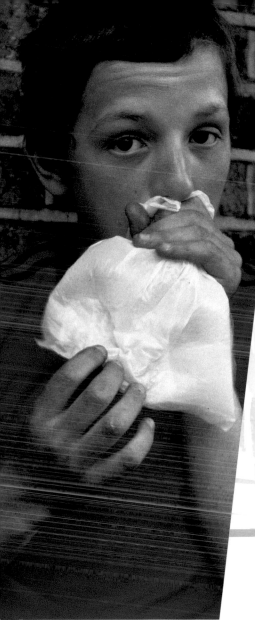

Some definitions

Solvents:

liquids that easily dissolve other substances. They are found in products such as glue, paint stripper, correction fluid thinner and dry-cleaning fluid. They may be abused by people who inhale the vapours that they give off.

Volatile substances:

substances that rapidly give off vapours, or gases at ordinary room temperature. This group includes all the solvents as mentioned above, plus gas fuels and propellants in aerosols.

Inhalants:

any volatile substance that is breathed in for the purpose of intoxication, or getting 'high'.

... and abuse

Sniffing glue is one kind of solvent abuse. Solvents are easier for young people to obtain than alcohol and drugs, but are no less harmful.

Deaths from solvents gave rise to a large number of sensational press headlines in the 1980s, coinciding with crazes for glue-sniffing and petrol-sniffing in Europe and North America. Although these headlines later gave way to stories about street drugs such as ecstasy and heroin, an alarming number of people still die from solvent abuse every year; it simply is not being reported as often in the media. Many teenagers are shocked to hear that young people just like them die every week from inhaling these chemicals. It is also hard to get the message across that solvents kill more people every year than several of the illegal street drugs do.

Who abuses solvents?

The greatest number of deaths and injuries related to solvents happen to young teenagers. People in this age group are more likely than others to experiment, to try looking for new and extreme experiences, and to be unable to resist pressure from their peers. Young teenagers are also the most likely to ignore safety warnings, or not fully understand what their risky behaviour can lead to. In addition, they have ready access to solvents, whereas they are less able to obtain intoxicating substances such as alcohol or illegal drugs.

Many drug education programmes aimed at this age group do not contain very much information about gases, glues and aerosols, perhaps because of worries that they may encourage 'copycat' behaviour. Most people who try inhaling do so only once or twice, as part of a phase of experimenting, and then they never try again because they don't like it. Only a few people who experiment go on to abuse solvents on a regular basis.

Peer group
Friends can be great for fun times and support, but can be a source of pressure too.

What can be done?

Many manufacturers have been very responsible and have responded to reports that their products are being abused by reformulating or repackaging them. They have exchanged solvents for other chemicals that cannot be abused, added foul-smelling chemicals to glues to make them unpleasant to sniff, and included clear warnings on containers that the contents can kill if inhaled. Laws have also been passed to prevent shopkeepers from selling products to young people who are likely to abuse them.

The other main way to prevent solvent abuse is education, so that people know the true risks, and can choose to avoid this activity. Health centres, charities and other groups have also been set up to deal with the problem, and they give out information on the subject to teenagers, parents, schools and other organizations. They may also provide counselling or other services for anyone who has become dependent on solvents and wants to give up, or they may be able to refer them to nearby specialist treatment centres.

'A few of the kids in my class have tried inhalants maybe once or twice, but most of us can't be bothered. If they are as good as some people say, then why do most teenagers never use them?'
(Tom, aged 15)

About this book

Although gases, glues and aerosols are often forgotten when drug statistics are being compiled, or drug education is being given, it is very important for everyone to understand the true dangers of abuse. It is very easy to underestimate how deadly these chemicals can be, especially if the products that contain them are lying around the house and appear harmless at first sight. This book aims to give a clear picture of solvent abuse and the damage it can do.

Chapter 1 looks at the different types of solvents, the immediate effects of abuse, and the law. Chapter 2 examines the people around the world who abuse solvents, and how many of them die every year. Chapters 3 and 4 examine the real risks of solvent misuse, including sudden death and addiction. In Chapter 5, the tell-tale signs of solvent abuse are discussed, and there is a checklist of what to do in a solvent-related emergency. At the back of the book there is a list of useful resources, and a glossary to explain some of the less familiar words.

1 What are solvents?
Types of solvents and their effects

Solvent abuse is deliberately inhaling (breathing in) the fumes from certain household or industrial products in order to get intoxicated, or 'high'. It's sometimes called 'sniffing' or 'huffing'. When glues or gases are used, people may just say they're 'doing glue', 'sniffing glue' or 'doing gas'. Terms such as 'glue-sniffing', 'solvent abuse', 'inhalant misuse', 'recreational solvent use' and 'volatile substance abuse' are all used to describe this activity.

Solvents and volatile substances

Solvents are chemicals, usually liquids, which are able to dissolve other substances. In this book, the term 'solvents' refers mainly to chemicals found in products such as glues (adhesives) and aerosols (spray cans) which cause intoxication or a 'high' when they are abused. Solvents can also be found in

Molecules

In solids, the molecules are tightly packed and cannot move around much, but can vibrate. In liquids, molecules can move around a little more; and in gases, molecules are far apart from one another. Solvents can change from liquid to gas very easily. Increased temperature makes molecules move further apart, turning liquid to gas. Increased pressure forces molecules closer together, turning gas to liquid.

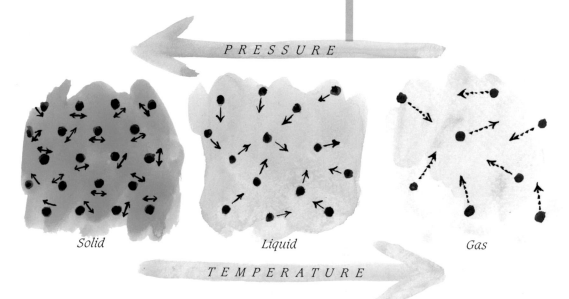

PRESSURE

Solid   Liquid   Gas

TEMPERATURE

Volatile substances

SOLVENTS

Includes chemicals found in certain brands of glues, nail polish and nail polish remover, petrol, dyes, cleaning fluids, de-greasing agents, correction fluid and thinners, paints and paint stripper and dry-cleaning fluids.

AEROSOL PROPELLANTS

Ingredients found in some cans of fly spray, deodorant, pain relief spray, spray paint, cleaning products, de-icer, air freshener and hair lacquer.

FUEL GASES

Found in lighter fluid canisters, camping gas cylinders and domestic gas supplies.

OTHER COMPOUNDS

This includes anaesthetics, nitrous oxide and 'room odourizers'.

Aerosol
Aerosol sprays are powered by volatile substances.

dry-cleaning fluids, household cleaning products, paint strippers and thinners, nail polish removers and typewriter correction fluids.

Solvents are volatile substances, usually small molecules known as hydrocarbons that contain carbon and hydrogen atoms. If they are kept cool, or under pressure, these tiny molecules move around more slowly and become packed more closely together, so the substances take on the form of solids or liquids. The term 'volatile' means that the molecules easily move away from each other to become gases, or liquids that give off vapours, when they're at room temperature.

As well as solvents, some other volatile substances including certain fuel gases and anaesthetics are abused to get similar effects. The term 'volatile substance abuse' (VSA) is therefore strictly more accurate than 'solvent abuse'. The commonest products in cases of volatile substance abuse are fuel gases, glues and aerosols.

The physical properties of volatile substances give them a wide range of uses in everyday life. Solvents in glue and paint allow these products to dry faster because most of the liquid in them vaporizes quickly once it's out of the container. Paint thinners dissolve into the paint and mix smoothly with it, making it thinner and runnier. When used in aerosol containers, volatile

Aerosol spray

Gas under
pressure

Valve

Liquid and
gas solution

Tube

Roll it on
Solvents make paint easier to use, but good ventilation is essential for safety.

How an aerosol works
The propellant gas is stored under pressure. The valve at the top of the can opens when pressed, and the contents are forced out through the nozzle in a fine spray.

substances work as a propellant, allowing the contents of the can to be sprayed out evenly. Industrial cleaners dissolve grease or remove oil-based paints, and dry-cleaning fluids remove stains and take dirt out of clothing. Fuel gases are used in lighters and camping gas cylinders because they are flammable, in other words they catch on fire very easily.

The average household in Europe or the USA contains more than 30 products that have potential for volatile substance abuse. Many of these are in daily use and are not locked away, although many of them are clearly labelled as being dangerous to inhale.

Not much of a party

'We used to have lots of parties at my mate Pete's house when his parents were out. Most of my schoolmates used to go along. The last time I went there were four lads who went off to a room upstairs and started messing around with cans of deodorant, and anything they could get hold of from around the house. It really stank the place out and they looked like idiots, staggering around and shouting. They were probably trying to impress the girls, but they didn't get very far.

They said Pete and I should try some because "everybody else was doing it", but there were only four of them. That's not what I'd call "everybody". We just laughed at them. Nobody else was interested. It's a bit dirty and disgusting really. I think it's something that immature little kids do, not someone our age.'
(Andy, aged 16)

The main substances abused

The fuel gases that are commonly abused are found in cigarette lighter refills and camping gas cylinders. They mostly contain a gas called butane, or one called propane, and they are highly flammable. About 90 per cent of what's contained inside a cigarette lighter refill is pressurized butane gas in liquid form. When the butane gas is at room temperature, the molecules in it are spread far apart from one another, but when it is cooled or placed under pressure, this pushes the molecules much closer together and makes the butane behave more like a liquid. Butane in cigarette lighter refills is said to be responsible for between 31 and 50 per cent of all solvent abuse deaths in Europe and North America each year, most of which are instant deaths. These figures vary from country to country, and from year to year.

Butane
Up to 50 per cent of solvent abuse deaths are caused by butane in lighter refills.

Glues come in several different forms, such as woodworking adhesives, contact adhesives, rubber repair cement and many others. Contact adhesives are thought to be involved in half of all glue-sniffing deaths. They contain several different solvents, but the commonest one is called toluene. A significant number of deaths caused by toluene abuse happen when people have accidents, such as falls or being hit by cars, while under the influence. Overall, glues are thought to cause between 7 and 18 per cent of solvent-related deaths every year.

'I thought inhaling lighter fuel would be the safest, because it's fairly pure. But now I know it's the most dangerous thing to try, which came as a nasty surprise.'
(Barney, aged 14)

Aerosols are responsible for approximately 14 to 19 per cent of VSA-related deaths, and a large portion of those are due to sniffing from deodorant cans. Commonly abused products include certain brands of hairspray, anti-perspirants and deodorants, pain relief spray, fly spray, air freshener and spray paints. The chemical used most often is butane, which is used as a propellant to help force out the liquid inside the can in a steady and even spray.

Righting a wrong
Many schools and colleges have banned brands of correction fluid that are abusable.

Other commonly abused volatile substances are found in certain commercial typing correction fluids and thinners (trichloroethylene), nail polish remover (acetone and esters), some paints and paint thinners, and paint strippers. This long list of products with potential for abuse also includes petrol, dry-cleaning fluids and spot removers, anaesthetics (ether and nitrous oxide), 'room odourizers' (isobutyl nitrite and similar substances), industrial whipped cream dispensers (nitrous oxide again), plaster remover and a few shoe and metal polishes.

Solvents in the workplace

Solvents are very common in a variety of workplaces, and strict health and safety regulations exist to protect workers from their harmful effects. Each of these volatile substances may have direct toxic effects, and the other chemicals they are mixed with can cause poisoning too. In the UK, it is estimated that around eight million workers are exposed to solvents at work every year, and two million of these people are exposed to solvents on a regular basis.

Printing ink
*Print workers are
at high risk of
being exposed to
solvents.*

Painters, decorators, printers
and dry-cleaners are all workers
who are at a high risk of being
exposed to solvents. Volatile
substances are found in industrial
products such as paints, inks and thinners, and because
they are so widespread it's sometimes easy to take them
for granted and forget to handle them with the proper care.
While most people are exposed to solvents accidentally,
occasionally someone may be deliberately abusing the
products. For example, a few people who work in operating
theatres or dental surgeries have been caught abusing
anaesthetic gases.

Industrial exposure has been linked to a number of serious
health problems. Usually, someone is exposed to a low
dose of the chemical on a very regular basis, sometimes
over a period of many years. It can be accidentally inhaled
from the air or absorbed through the skin, depending upon
the product.

Low-intensity exposure to certain solvents has been linked
with damage to cells in the liver, heart, lungs and kidneys.

The liver and kidneys are very active organs that process and remove many toxins (poisonous substances) from the body, so they are essential for good health. If the damage is spotted soon enough, and further exposure to solvents is completely prevented, most people will make a full recovery, but if someone is exposed to these solvents for a very long period of time, these effects can become irreversible. It has also been suggested that exposure to some solvents can damage muscle tissue, and stop the bone marrow working properly, so that not enough red and white blood cells are produced for a person to stay healthy.

Solvents can also cause harm to the nervous system, including encephalitis (inflammation of the brain), difficulty in balancing and walking, and damage to the nerves in the arms and legs. Some solvents, such as petrol, have carcinogenic (cancer-causing) powers, and often contain other toxic substances that can cause poisoning, such as lead. Solvents are thought to have caused liver cancer in a small number of people.

There is some evidence to suggest that exposure to volatile substances in pregnancy can increase the risk of miscarriage or cause abnormalities in the unborn baby. Paints, inks and thinners have been linked to low sperm counts in men, and the greater the exposure, the higher the risk. Direct contact with solvents on the skin can cause chronic irritations such as dermatitis and contact eczema, which can be hard to treat.

Businesses make it safer for their workforces when they provide safety training, good ventilation (extractor fans taking out fumes), clear labelling and warnings on dangerous products, and regular health checks. If a doctor thinks that workers have been exposed to solvents, samples of blood, urine and exhaled air (breath) can be tested. Safe limits have been set for exposure to many solvents.

Giving gas
People who work with anaesthetics are taught to handle them with care and respect.

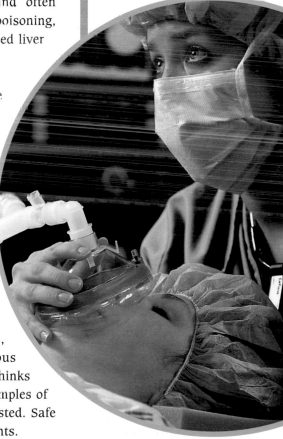

Deliberate abuse

Deliberate volatile substance abuse happens in many ways, but these are the most common ones:

⦿ Clear liquids are often poured onto a rag, a handkerchief, or part of a person's clothing such as their sleeve or lapel. As they give off fumes, these are sniffed. There is commonly a tell-tale chemical smell that lingers on clothing after it has been used in this way.

'My teacher caught me sniffing correction fluid thinners during a lesson. It's a clear liquid and I dabbed some on my sleeve, so I thought I wouldn't get spotted. But I wasn't as clever as I thought, because the smell gave it away when she walked past.'
(Marie, aged 13)

⦿ Thicker liquids such as paints are often left in their original container, or transferred to smaller pots or jars. The lid is taken off and the vapours are inhaled.

Aerosol abuse

Aerosols are sometimes sprayed into a bag before they are inhaled.

⊚ Sticky substances such as glues are often poured into plastic bags such as crisp packets or freezer bags. The bags are usually held over the mouth and nose, and are sometimes warmed to make the vapours come out quicker. Glue-sniffing is often a group activity, with the bags being passed around the group.

⊚ Aerosols and gases are sometimes sprayed into a bag and inhaled, or are squirted straight into the mouth. Sprays containing products such as foams, gels and mousses are not usually abused.

All these methods of abuse are dangerous, but squirting aerosols and gases right into the mouth or throat is one of the most likely causes of death to recreational users.

Solvents and the law

Solvents are so common in household and workplace products that it would be almost impossible to ban them all. Unlike most street drugs, solvents are legal to possess in the UK, whatever your age. It is not illegal to sniff or inhale these substances, even though they are often more deadly than illegal drugs (also known as 'controlled substances'). Just because the products involved are legal, it doesn't mean that they are a safe alternative to street drugs.

'I work in a hardware shop on Saturdays. The police and the manager have been working together recently, and I know I'd lose my job if I sold cans of glue to underage kids.'
(Cherry, aged 19)

In Britain strict laws apply to the sale of solvents. A shopkeeper can be taken to court for selling solvents to someone who is likely to abuse them. For example, it is an offence to supply a cigarette lighter refill containing butane to anyone under the age of 18, as this age group are the most likely to abuse the product. England, Northern Ireland and Wales are covered by the Cigarette Lighter Refill (Safety) Regulations 1999 and the Intoxicating Substances Supply Act 1985. A retailer who breaks the rules can face a large fine or a six-month prison sentence.

In Scotland, the law is slightly different. Under Scottish Common Law, it is criminal conduct to supply or sell solvents to any person, knowing that the substances will be abused. For example, shopkeepers are warned not to sell glues to teenagers who seem to be intoxicated already. Also, under the Solvent Abuse (Scotland) Act of 1983, a young person who abuses solvents can be referred to the Children's Panel. The young person will not be charged with any offence. The Panel is there to assess and help them, not to give them a criminal conviction.

Desired effects of intoxication

When volatile substances are deliberately inhaled to cause intoxication, the vapours go into the lungs and quickly enter the bloodstream through the thin lung tissues. Once in the bloodstream they are taken to the brain and nerves in less than one minute, and it is here that they have the most effect. Solvents act as central nervous system depressants: they slow down brain activity. The degree of the intoxication and how long it lasts are affected by the substance that's being used, how deeply it is inhaled and how often.

The first sensation is usually euphoria, which is a feeling of excitement, a 'high' or a 'rush'. The feelings of euphoria last for somewhere between two minutes and one hour, depending on which substance is being used. The effects of glues last longer than the effects of gases. Users sometimes repeat the process of inhaling to stay high when the feelings of euphoria start to wear off.

alveoli

heart

lungs

How solvents reach the brain

Inhaled solvent vapours are drawn deep into the lungs, and quickly reach tiny air sacs called alveoli (shown magnified). The alveoli are very thin and surrounded by blood vessels, and the solvents pass straight into the blood, then to the heart and brain, within seconds.

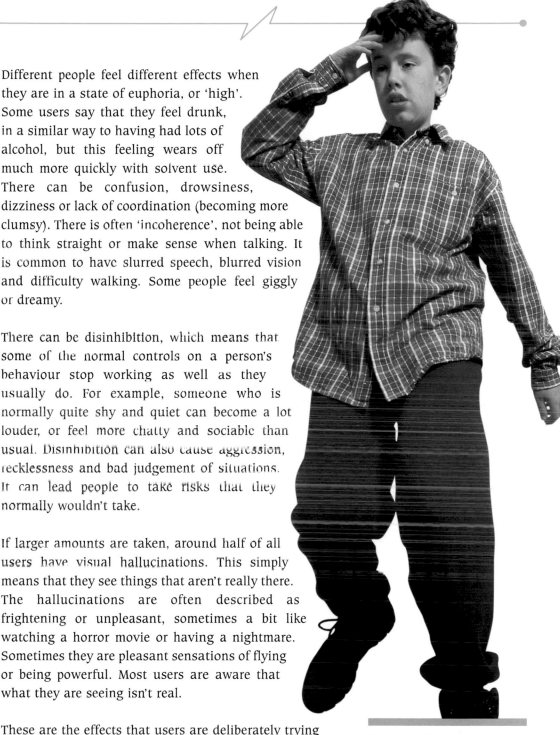

Different people feel different effects when they are in a state of euphoria, or 'high'. Some users say that they feel drunk, in a similar way to having had lots of alcohol, but this feeling wears off much more quickly with solvent use. There can be confusion, drowsiness, dizziness or lack of coordination (becoming more clumsy). There is often 'incoherence', not being able to think straight or make sense when talking. It is common to have slurred speech, blurred vision and difficulty walking. Some people feel giggly or dreamy.

There can be disinhibition, which means that some of the normal controls on a person's behaviour stop working as well as they usually do. For example, someone who is normally quite shy and quiet can become a lot louder, or feel more chatty and sociable than usual. Disinhibition can also cause aggression, recklessness and bad judgement of situations. It can lead people to take risks that they normally wouldn't take.

If larger amounts are taken, around half of all users have visual hallucinations. This simply means that they see things that aren't really there. The hallucinations are often described as frightening or unpleasant, sometimes a bit like watching a horror movie or having a nightmare. Sometimes they are pleasant sensations of flying or being powerful. Most users are aware that what they are seeing isn't real.

These are the effects that users are deliberately trying to get by 'sniffing'. There are many unwanted effects and dangers too, which are covered in detail in Chapter 3. The unpleasant effects last much longer then the feelings of euphoria, and the main risk is death.

In a spin
Dizziness and lack of coordination increase the risk of falls and other accidents.

2 Patterns of use
Solvents around the world

Solvent abuse is not such a recent problem. In the USA and the UK between 1799 and the mid-1840s there was a fashion for inhaling newly-discovered laughing gas (nitrous oxide) and ether vapours at parties, especially among wealthy people. There were even stage shows and exhibitions where people in the audience could inhale these volatile substances, or be amused by the sight of other people in intoxicated states. Eventually these practices fell from favour, and nitrous oxide gained a legitimate use as a dental anaesthetic in 1844, after a dentist named Horace Wells saw the effects of the gas being demonstrated at a circus sideshow.

Often, people who have easy access to volatile substances have tried inhaling them, from medical students with ether that was meant for use as an anaesthetic, to soldiers with petrol that was meant to power military vehicles. Several examples of petrol-sniffing among teenagers were reported by the press in the USA in the 1950s, and the first case of reported solvent abuse in the UK was in 1962. There were crazes for glue-sniffing in both countries in the late 1970s and early 1980s, some of which was linked with punk music and fashions. Media coverage in Western countries reached a peak in the 1980s, but this tailed off when papers started to run more and more stories about drugs such as heroin and ecstasy instead. Even though it isn't in the news as often, volatile substance abuse is still happening, and young people continue to die from it.

Laughing gas
This early nineteenth-century cartoon was entitled 'An Experimental Lecture on the Powers of Air'. Scientists are shown demonstrating the disinhibiting effects of nitrous oxide.

1950s ▶

Juveniles with gasoline fever

Gas station 'kicks'
LOCAL gas station attendants have been dismissed after sniffing gasoline fumes for kicks. Owner Kyle Watts says he has never seen anything like it …

Craze reaches the UK

LONDON youngsters have been caught inhaling petrol fumes, copying their American cousins.

Maniac factory worker

A man has been removed from his post after being caught abusing industrial cleaning fluids. Doctors say he will probably go blind or die from poisoning.

◀ 1960s

Punks menace city centre

PUNK rockers, high on glue, have gone on the rampage in several towns, stealing from shops and terrifying local residents.

Stop this outrage

Fights broke out between intoxicated skinhead gang members, whose drug of choice is cheap glue. There is a rising tide of violence and thuggery on our streets…

1970s ▶

Deadly craze for 'sniffing' sweeps the nation

More and more schoolchildren are playing truant to sniff glue and drink cheap alcohol.

Ban sales of glue to youngsters

Parents call for new legislation to put a stop to the deadly habit that destroys young minds and lives.

Poisonous cargo

A campaign group says teenagers in a small town in Lancashire are sniffing enough glue in one week to fill a petrol tanker.

◀ 1980s

Charity warns of summer sniffing deaths

Residents are warned to be more aware of the increase in inhalant abuse that occurs in the summer months, mainly in parks or by railway lines.

Hidden epidemic

One in 50 deaths in the 15 to 19 age group is a direct result of volatile substance abuse, but why is nothing being done about it?

2000s ▶

Common patterns of abuse

The most common age for experimenting with solvents is around 13 or 14 years old, and it's relatively rare in under-11s. Boys seem slightly more likely to try solvents than girls, and it seems to be more common in inner-city areas. But there is no stereotypical user; users can come from any social, racial or cultural background.

Most teenagers never experiment with solvents, and the majority of those that do generally try it only once or twice and decide they don't like it. 'Glue-sniffing' seems to go in and out of fashion at different times, and there are often local crazes in particular schools, or towns and counties, commonly during the summer holidays when students are not in school.

School truants are twice as likely to have tried solvents as children who attend school regularly. Regular volatile substance users are more likely to say that they feel alienated from other people, or that they hate their teachers, than those who do not use these substances. It's hard to say whether this is a cause or an effect of solvent abuse.

School's out

Glue-sniffing is often done in groups, in a park or derelict area, and groups may get together like this especially during school holidays.

VSA around the world

In a survey in 2001 of British secondary school students aged 11 to 15, 7 per cent reported that they had used solvents in the past year. About 20 per cent of them said they had been offered glue or gas in the previous 12 months, suggesting that more than half of them had felt able to say no.

In the European Union, the UK is the country with the highest levels of volatile substance abuse (most studies say between 7 and 10 per cent of young people have tried it), followed closely by Sweden. Abuse is slightly less common in Italy, Denmark, France and Greece, where around 6 per cent of young people are thought to have tried it. The countries where inhalant use is the least common are Portugal, Finland and Spain, where researchers say only around 3 per cent of young people have ever tried solvents.

In the USA, a number of studies of high school students have found that between 15 and 20 per cent of them admit to ever having used solvents. Children as young as six years old have admitted to inhaling. There seems to be considerable variation from area to area, and in particular there seems to be a higher rate of inhalant use among young people in isolated Native American communities, and possibly among those of Hispanic origin. Laws on the use of solvents, and their production and sales vary from state to state.

An unpleasant experience

Sarah tried sniffing glue twice when she was 14. Both times she was on her own in her bedroom and used glue that she'd taken from her Dad's tool kit. She says that she was bored and looking for something exciting to do. The effects of the glue didn't last for long, and afterwards she had terrible headaches, felt tired, and had sore eyes and throat. She says it was just a phase that she was going through, and she probably won't try it again.

Inhalant use has also been reported in Australia and New Zealand, and seems to be more of a problem among young Native Australians (Aboriginals) living in remote areas. There are also reports of problem use in Asia, Japan and Africa. Because it is often kept secret, it is hard to know how widespread volatile substance abuse has truly become.

There are thought to be around 100 million street children worldwide. They are homeless, often orphans, and the situation is worst in poorer countries such as Paraguay, Guatemala, Tanzania, Uganda, the Philippines, Bolivia and parts of Eastern Europe. It is estimated that 85 per cent of street children in Paraguay have used volatile substances, mainly petrol and glue. In Guatemala, more than half of all homeless children are thought to use solvents regularly, mainly shoe glue from local factories. In Brazil, there are reports of secretly prepared mixtures of volatile substances being sold for the specific purpose of abuse.

A means of escape?

Many street children abuse solvents to escape the misery of their living conditions.

Street children often use intoxication as an escape from the grim world of poverty and deprivation that they live in. Users often say that the solvents dull feelings of hunger, and give a sensation of warmth that takes their minds off the cold and helps them get to sleep when they are sleeping outside. Many of them quickly become dependent upon these substances.

Volatile substance deaths

The main risk of volatile substance abuse is death, which usually happens suddenly, without warning. Out of all the people known to have died from solvent abuse in the UK, the youngest was 9 and the oldest was 76. Most deaths worldwide are in young people under the age of 20 (around 70 per cent), and the majority of those who die are male (over 80 per cent). Many of the people who die are first-time users, and no previous history of abuse can be detected in around 40 per cent of solvent related deaths.

In the UK there is a study group that looks at all VSA-related deaths. They noted that the number of deaths rose in the 1980s and reached a peak (151) in 1990. The overall numbers of deaths fell after a Department of Health awareness campaign, and in 2001 enforcement of bans on lighter fuel caused a 60 per cent reduction in deaths of teenagers. On average, five people in the UK die from volatile substance abuse every month, and around half of them are teenagers.

'After my son died from inhaling lighter fuel, I kept going over it in my mind. I didn't see any of the signs. Perhaps I could have saved him if I'd known.'
(Rita, aged 40)

Why do people try solvents?

Friends who use solvents

It's perfectly normal for teenagers to desperately want to be the same as their friends, and this is a time in their lives when it seems especially important to 'fit in' with their social group. Often they will follow the lead of a dominant person, or copy the behaviour of someone they admire, even if deep down they're not so sure that it's the best thing to do. Some people subtly pressurize their friends to try things, or tease or bully them to get them to join in.

Look-alikes
It's tempting to copy friends, just to fit in with the group.

⊛ Curiosity

It's natural to be curious about something you don't know much about, especially if other people are talking about it in a positive light. Many young people simply have the desire to experiment and try all kinds of new experiences, especially if they think it will have an interesting or pleasurable effect.

'I'm the kind of person who will try anything once, to see what it's like. Sometimes it gets me into trouble, like when the police caught me sniffing glue and took me home to my angry parents.'
(Casey, aged 14)

⊛ Excitement and danger

It's human nature to seek out a little excitement, and many people find that forbidden or illegal things have a thrill about them. Some people like to try things that others might find unsettling or frightening. Gases and glues are sometimes shoplifted too, which can be part of the same behaviour pattern.

To shock

As part of growing up and becoming more independent, it is common to go through a rebellious phase, or to do extreme things to assert your individuality. Using solvents can make a strong statement that's designed to shock a parent, a teacher or other adults.

Escape

Some solvent users get 'high' to blot out bad feelings and temporarily get away from unpleasant things in their lives. This can happen when there are problems such as bullying, family difficulties or abuse. Inhaling can become a way of dealing with problems on a regular basis, and dependency (psychological addiction) can begin like this.

Experimenting

Teenagers often experiment with shocking behaviour or appearances. Sometimes it's harmless fun and sometimes it's more risky.

Control

Solvent abuse may give a user a false sense of control or power over their own life. Many 'sniffers' report being able to control their hallucinations. Some street children in very poor countries say they use glue to control feelings of hunger when they cannot afford enough to eat.

Boredom

Solvent abuse is often a social activity, and sometimes users get into it because they think there's nothing better to do. Lone users may also say they sniff to fill up empty hours of their day.

◉ Easy to get hold of

As mentioned before, the average household contains over 30 products that might be misused, and most parents do not have much knowledge about what or where the dangerous substances may be. Young people generally find it easier to get hold of volatile substances than it is to buy alcohol, tobacco or street drugs. If something is lying around it is more tempting than something that is hard to buy.

◉ Not illegal to possess or use in many countries

It is sometimes hard to explain the dangers of solvent abuse to people who say that they are not breaking the law and so they are 'doing nothing wrong'.

Learning to stand up for himself

William let his friends talk him into inhaling lighter fuel, but he really didn't want to do it. They were by a disused railway line, and two of them got out plastic bags and gas canisters from their bags. When they offered him some he said no, but they started laughing at him and calling him names. William got really embarrassed and gave in to them to shut them up.

He was scared that they'd think he was a 'chicken' or a wimp, so he just went along with it, trying to act like a 'hard man'. He wishes he had been more able to stand up to them, feels a bit stupid for giving in to it, and is annoyed at himself for being so weak-willed. He thinks next time things will be different, but says it isn't always easy standing up for himself.

How to cope with peer pressure

Nobody has the right to force you to use solvents if you don't want to.

Real friends will respect your wishes and decisions, so think long and hard about whether you want to be friends with people who don't.

Remember that other people in the group may not really want to use solvents either, but may be less able than you to stand up for themselves.

Remain relaxed and friendly, but point out your reasons for not joining in. There are several good reasons for avoiding inhalants.

Continued use of solvents

Of all the young people who try solvents, only about 10 per cent will carry on (usually for a short time in a group of friends as 'recreational' users) and less than 1 per cent will become frequent and heavy users. These very heavy users are often in their early 20s and are more likely to be male. They develop tolerance to the chemicals, and need to inhale more and more to get the same effect. They may end up psychologically dependent upon solvents. This dependency seems to be more likely in young people who start using solvents as a way of coping with, or blocking out, unpleasant feelings or situations.

'We used to sniff glue in the park at the weekend and in the school holidays. Most of us got bored after a while but one guy kept trying to make us do it one more time.'
(Tasha, aged 15)

Users who continue to sniff heavily and for a long period of time often end up doing so on their own. If they started sniffing with a group of friends, these other friends usually grow out of the habit quite quickly. Users become generally run down, depressed and tired, their work or studies can suffer, and so can their personal relationships. Some of them go on to become dependent on alcohol or other drugs.

3 Solvent dangers
The real risks of inhalants

Volatile substance abuse has both short-term and long-term unpleasant side effects, even though the 'buzz' or 'high' may last for only a few minutes. The main risk with solvents is sudden death, and it is impossible to predict who will die or when. A person using solvents for the first time is just as likely to die as someone who has already used them for many months.

There are no effective precautions that can be taken to avoid the risk of sudden death. Although some methods of inhaling are far more risky than others, the underlying danger still remains. The only way to avoid the risk of death is to stay away from solvents altogether.

No risk reduction
All methods of inhaling solvents carry danger. Here someone is sniffing vapours from a rag.

One piece of good news is that, with the right help and support, young experimental users who stop inhaling solvents soon enough will nearly all make a good recovery from the ill effects, without any severe or lasting damage to their health. This may not be the case with heavy users who continue for years, however.

It is hard to find accurate statistics, partly because of the secretive nature of solvent abuse, and partly because many of the risks that are commonly linked to volatile substance abuse are based on studies that are out-of-date, or not relevant to teenage users. This chapter explores the real dangers of getting high on gases, glues and aerosols, without the hype that sometimes surrounds the subject.

'My teacher said I would die from brain damage if I used solvents, but he didn't tell me I might throw up or get nosebleeds. My friends say it's safe when I know it makes them ill. Who do I trust?'
(Blue, aged 15)

What makes it risky?

When substances such as alcohol, street drugs or solvents are used to cause intoxication, there are always some risks. These risks are governed by three main factors: what the substance is and how it is taken, the person who is taking it, and their current environment.

Substance-related factors

Solvents rapidly affect the nervous system, heart and lungs. Like many drugs, they may lead to psychological dependence if they are used regularly. Some dangers are associated with how often the solvents are used, and how much is inhaled each time. Certain ways of inhaling or sniffing the substances are more dangerous than others: for example, sniffing gases directly from pressurized canisters or inhaling glue vapours from a bag pulled completely over the face. Even if these methods of abuse are avoided, the risk of sudden death is always still there.

User-related factors

Many people have underlying health problems, even though they may not be aware of them and feel fit and well. Anyone with a heart condition, kidney or liver disease, or lung problems including asthma, should stay away from solvents. Lack of knowledge of the effects can cause distress or panic when unfamiliar sensations arise, and intoxication can lead to riskier behaviour than usual. Mental health problems such as stress, anxiety or depression can lead people to use solvents heavily as a means of escape, but solvent abuse can make these feelings even more unpleasant.

Out of the way
Sniffing alone in isolated places is one of the riskiest ways to abuse solvents.

Environmental factors

Dangerous, derelict or remote environments are often favoured because users want secrecy so that they won't be disturbed. Accidents are more likely to occur by rivers, roads or train tracks. Operating machinery, cycling or driving a car under the influence increases the possibility of injury. Other people who are around may encourage someone to inhale more than they thought they would, or may try to take advantage of their intoxicated state.

Short-term effects of solvents

Gases, glues and aerosols are inhaled by recreational users to get themselves into an intoxicated state. There are several unpleasant short-term side effects that happen along with this, including facial reddening, nausea and vomiting, unpleasant or frightening hallucinations, and irritation of the skin, eyes, ears, nose and throat as the body tries to rid itself of the toxic substances. Inhaling can also cause unexpected deaths in several ways.

'I sniffed so much in a day once that it made me cough up blood. It's not hard to identify someone who has been doing this stuff, it makes your face all red.'
(James, aged 16)

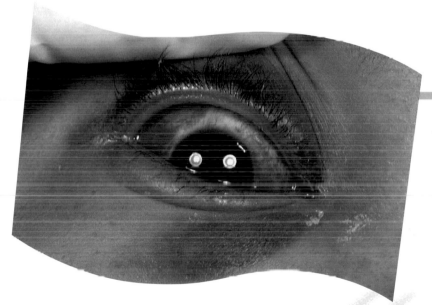

Inflammation
Inflammation of the mucous membrane at the front of the eye is called conjunctivitis.

Shortly after the intoxication has worn off, users can have problems with headaches, sore skin, conjunctivitis (irritation, watering and reddening of the delicate surface of the eyeball), coughing, painful or dry mouth and throat, or blocked nose. Acne spots can be made worse, and unpleasant and smelly breath is common. There can also be similar sensations to an alcohol hangover, such as feeling sick, unable to concentrate, tired and miserable for several hours.

'I tried sniffing one brand of nail polish remover to get high. I wasn't that impressed and I had a banging headache for hours afterwards.'
(Helen, aged 14)

Sudden sniffing death

Sudden sniffing death can be caused by cardiac arrhythmia (irregular heartbeat), cardiac arrest (the heart stops beating) or respiratory depression (the lungs do not work fast enough).

Cardiac arrhythmia

When solvents are inhaled, they go into the lungs and quickly enter the bloodstream. The blood is pumped around the body and carries the solvents to the tissues, reaching the heart muscle and brain within seconds. Solvents are thought to make heart muscle cells (also known as the myocardium) unusually sensitive to the exciting effects of the stress hormone adrenaline, and to stimulation from nearby nerves that travel down from the brain.

In a healthy heart, the myocardium contracts and relaxes in a smooth and well-coordinated way, pushing blood effectively to the body and lungs. The blood carries oxygen to all the body's tissues, keeping them alive. Solvents sometimes disrupt the smooth action of the myocardium, making different muscle cells around the heart begin to contract in the wrong order. This means that the heart is unable to contract and relax properly, and cannot pump the blood around the body so efficiently. This situation is called a cardiac arrhythmia, and is very dangerous because in its most extreme form the brain and other body tissues quickly become starved of oxygen, which can be deadly. Cardiac arrhythmias are probably responsible for over half of all solvent-related deaths.

Once a serious arrhythmia has developed, the victim cannot be saved by normal first aid methods such as mouth-to-mouth resuscitation. Special emergency medical

Adrenaline

Adrenaline is the 'fight or flight' hormone that allows us to respond to stressful situations where we might need to take action or run away. One of its main actions is to make the heart beat stronger and faster. This gets more blood pumping to the muscles, allowing them to work more quickly.

equipment is needed, and this does not always arrive in time. The risk of developing a sudden arrhythmia continues for a few hours after someone has stopped inhaling the volatile substance.

Because the heart muscle cells are in a state where they are too sensitive to the stress hormone adrenaline, a sudden shock can kill. This can be caused by shouting at an intoxicated person, having an argument with them, grabbing or shaking them or chasing them. All of these actions cause a surge of adrenaline to be released into the bloodstream, causing a fatal arrhythmia.

Cardiac arrest

Some people, even some who are young and appear to be perfectly fit, have an underlying heart defect of which they are not aware. It could be a slightly unusual rhythm of their heartbeat, a hole in the wrong place between the chambers of their heart, misshapen heart valves, or an unusual pattern of arteries or veins. The extra strain that solvent abuse places on their heart and circulation could push them into a critical state, causing a cardiac arrest.

Respiratory depression

Respiratory depression happens when the solvents enter the brain and directly affect the central nervous system by disrupting messages between the nerve cells in the brain and spine. These nerve messages normally make sure that someone is breathing deeply and regularly, and getting enough oxygen into their blood and body tissues. Solvents may slow down the rate of breathing so much that the sniffer dies from lack of oxygen.

Rouse them gently

If you find someone who is drowsy, remember that it could be dangerous to shake them or shout at them. You should try to wake them gently.

'One time I inhaled too much and I had an astonishing pain in my chest. I could feel my heart racing and I nearly passed out. I was terrified that I was damaged inside.'
(Johnny, aged 17)

Cold injuries

Gases and aerosols can be extremely cold when they come out of their canisters, because they have been stored under pressure and are released at a very low temperature. This makes them very harmful to human tissues, and there have been recorded cases of frostbite to hands and fingers just from opening canisters of certain volatile substances. The most dangerous cold injuries are ones where the throat or lungs are affected.

vagus nerve

When gases such as lighter fuel are squirted straight into the mouth there is a sudden drop in temperature, which can be deadly. The super-cold spray may freeze tissues in the back of the throat, or affect the vagus nerve in the larynx area ('voice box'). After the inside of the throat is frozen there may be rapid tissue swelling, and this can partially or fully obstruct the upper airway, causing asphyxiation (suffocation).

The vagus nerve
This nerve runs from the base of the brain to the neck, chest and abdomen. It sends branches to the larynx (1), lungs (2), heart (3), liver (4), stomach (5) and kidneys (6).

The vagus nerve is part of a delicate system of nerves and hormones that allows 'fine-tuning' of the heart rate to match it to the body's rapidly changing needs. The nerve runs down behind the throat on its way to the gut. If this area of it is affected by cold, one of its branches sends signals to the heart, and can cause death by slowing the heartbeat down too much.

'One day I just woke up to the fact that I was trashing my body and it had to stop. I gave up solvents and started to eat right and get fit, and have never looked back.'
(Gary, aged 20)

Some recreational solvent users have died after cold injuries to their lungs. After they inhaled gas or aerosol straight from the canister, part of their lung tissue became frozen, and then their bodies responded to the injury by producing large amounts of fluid. Having too much fluid in their lungs prevented them from getting enough oxygen when they tried to breathe in, and this was fatal.

Choking

Nausea, or feeling sick, is a very common side effect of inhaling solvents, and there can sometimes be vomiting too. When this is combined with extreme drowsiness or unconsciousness, this can be deadly. The vomit blocks off the airway, preventing breathing. The only real way to avoid this kind of danger is never to inhale solvents at all. Certain brands of glue seem to cause the most nausea, but different people react in different ways to the whole range of solvents, so the effects on any one person are not easily predictable.

Several deaths are caused every year by users choking on their own vomit while they are passed out, especially if they are lying on their back when they are sick. People who go off on their own to remote places to sniff glue are at particular risk, because it may be hours before they are found. If someone survives inhaling their own vomit, they can be very ill afterwards due to the stomach acid damaging their lungs, or there may be lasting brain damage.

Suffocation

Several young people are found dead every year with a large plastic bag pulled completely over their face, containing a volatile substance. They inhale solvent fumes from the bottom of the bag, then lose consciousness and suffocate. This can also happen when someone is inhaling solvents under a blanket or other bedclothes.

Recovery position

If someone is very drowsy or unconscious, you should put them into the recovery position. Lie them on their left side, with their right arm and right leg bent. This means that if they vomit, there is less risk of them choking on it.

Fires

As mentioned in Chapter 1, the gases and vapours are highly flammable: in other words, they catch fire very easily, for instance if they come into contact with a lighted cigarette, an electrical spark or an open fire. If this happens, a person's skin may be burnt directly, or their clothing or surroundings may go up in flames. Death can happen because of severe burns on the body or because of the smoke and fumes that a fire creates. Smoke kills very quickly, sometimes in less than one minute. Inhaling solvents in an enclosed space is particularly dangerous if there is an accidental fire.

Accidents

Driving under the influence of alcohol is illegal all around the world. This is because alcohol makes drivers too careless and reckless, and it affects their ability to coordinate their movements and judge distances. A drunk driver also overestimates their ability to drive safely and react to situations quickly enough. Being in charge of a motor vehicle, such as a car or motorcycle, whilst under the influence of gases or glue has similar dangers, and also carries legal penalties. Using gases or glue and then riding a bicycle in traffic is also unsafe.

In control
You need to be alert and in control when you are riding a bike. Cycling under the influence of alcohol, drugs or solvents would put you and others in danger.

Fatal road accidents have happened when people who have been inhaling have wandered into traffic and been hit by cars, or simply misjudged the timing of a road crossing. It seems to be more common when certain types of gas have recently been inhaled. Similarly, people who go to out-of-the way areas near railway tracks, to sniff undisturbed, have stumbled into the paths of oncoming trains. Inhaling solvents in derelict buildings is also very dangerous.

Getting 'high' causes people to behave in other ways that can result in them being badly hurt or even killed. Some people have fallen into a canal, river or lake and drowned, and others have decided wrongly that it would be safe to go swimming and then got into difficulties in the water. Deaths have also happened after intoxication caused falls from windows, trees, bridges and the tops of tall buildings such as multi-storey car parks. Operating machinery while under the influence of gas or glue is risky too.

Solvents nearly killed me

'I'm no expert on drugs, but solvents nearly killed me, and it's amazing that they're legal. I got into glue in a really big way when I was 12, and used to do loads of it with my mates. Looking back, I think I was trying to blot out all the horrible things in my life at the time, like family problems. We used to take so much that we almost blacked out.

One evening we were in the park doing glue and I started to feel more sick and drowsy than usual. The last thing I remember was thinking "Oh no, I'm gonna be sick", and that's about it. My friends say they all panicked when I passed out and started vomiting.

When I woke up someone had put me in the recovery position and I had sick all over my top. I was really lucky that a passer-by knew about first aid, and I'm glad I don't remember most of what happened – it's too scary to think about.'
(Katy, aged 15)

Personal safety

Getting 'high' can seriously affect personal judgement, and make someone less inhibited (reserved, or in control of their actions) than usual. This can lead to making mistakes about where to go and what to do, and who is trustworthy. Someone who is intoxicated can end up in disagreements or fights that they would never normally get involved in. Reduced levels of consciousness also make it easier for someone to be robbed, mugged, physically attacked or sexually assaulted, simply because they are not able to pick up on some of the danger signals or get away quickly enough.

'I knew I was getting in over my head when I threw a bottle at my sister. She's my best friend and only asked if I was OK. I think sniffing thinners made me act all weird.'
(Luke, aged 17)

Can the risks be reduced?

It must be clearly pointed out that there is always a risk of sudden death when any kind of solvent is used. This is regardless of who is using it, how or where. There is no way of removing the possibility of this kind of danger. However, other types of solvent-related deaths can be made less likely using harm minimization techniques. Obviously it would be best if volatile substance abuse were avoided altogether, but if someone insists on doing it then it's very hard to stop them, because the products are so easily available.

Talking it over
Drug counsellors provide information and a confidential place to talk.

What is harm minimization?

Some officials and counsellors who work with drug users follow a school of thought known as 'harm reduction' or 'harm minimization'. They believe that certain people will always experiment, in spite of all the warnings, and that these people should therefore be made fully aware of the risks that they are taking. They think that, if someone insists on using a drug, it is very difficult or even impossible to stop them, but that it is sometimes possible to persuade them to use less risky methods.

One example of action based on this theory is needle exchange programmes, where heroin addicts can get clean needles, preventing the spread of blood-borne diseases such as HIV and hepatitis. Not everyone agrees with the theory of harm minimization. In fact, some people think it makes it easier for youngsters to abuse substances, or even puts ideas in their heads and tempts them to try things.

Harm minimization advice on solvents includes the following points. Users must avoid inhaling with bags placed completely over their faces, and should avoid areas with poor ventilation, in case of suffocation. Users should also stay away from open fires or lit cigarettes, to prevent burns. They should also choose not to inhale aerosols or gases such as butane straight from the canister, as this is a common cause of solvent-related death. Those who go to remote areas alone to sniff should understand that they are in genuine danger, and should be encouraged to stay away from derelict buildings, railway lines, canals and rivers, and rooftops.

'A kid from my school went missing a few months ago. After a massive search, the police found him in a boarded-up house with a glue bag over his head. You never think someone you know will die like that.'
(Jessica, aged 16)

Mixing solvents with alcohol or street drugs can kill. Mixing any drugs should always be avoided, because the effects are so unpredictable. Experimental use of solvents while on medication is very unwise, especially with drugs that have been prescribed for asthma and epilepsy, because of interactions in the lungs and brain.

Best friends

Last year Steven found his best friend, Mark, dead at the wheel of his car. He'd been waiting for a lift home with Mark and the car was parked right outside the college gates. Steven found Mark slumped over in the front seat and tried to rouse him, but to no effect. He quickly raised the alarm, but the paramedics were unable to resuscitate Mark.

They found a canister of lighter fuel in Mark's lap. At the inquest into his death, Steven heard that Mark had probably died suddenly when his heartbeat became too irregular. Steven says that he thinks about his best friend every day, and as much as he misses him, he still feels angry at him sometimes.

Steven and Mark had experimented a few times with solvents. Then Steven told Mark that he wasn't going to bother with them any more. Steven thought Mark had stopped too, but now he reckons that Mark must have secretly carried on using lighter fuel on his own.

Long-term problems

Most teenagers who try solvents do so once or twice, then decide they don't like it and stop. A very small number of users carry on inhaling in the long term. The people who continue inhaling often do so alone, rather than in groups of friends. Their friends often look down on them for their behaviour and start to reject them.

Until the 1970s, what was known about the long-term effects of exposure to solvents was mostly based on medical studies of people who had come into contact with low levels of volatile substances in their workplace, often for many hours each day, over periods of many days or months. Teenagers who use inhalants to get 'high' are exposed to the chemicals in a different way, usually large amounts of solvents for very short periods of time, and so the physical effects on them are not necessarily going to be the same.

More recent studies have looked at individuals, or small groups of young people, who inhale volatile substances to get high. Many of these studies show strong links between long-term solvent abuse and depression. Long-term abuse also seems to cause increased bronchial secretions (phlegm), chronic irritation of the passages inside the nose, ulcers in the nose and mouth, and bloodshot eyes. Poor appetite and weight loss are common, and the long-term user may have problems such as difficulty concentrating, severe tiredness, irritability and paranoia.

In a few cases, solvent abuse appears to have caused permanent damage to the kidneys, liver or heart. It may also cause nerve damage in the fingers and toes. It has been suggested that it causes brain damage, although not all the evidence supports this. If someone who has engaged in short-term experimental or recreational use gives up sniffing completely, most of the unpleasant side effects go away after a few weeks, as the body clears out all the traces of solvent.

Dan's tragedy

Gemma's cousin, Dan, died after trying solvents for the first time. His mum found him lying on his bed. At first she thought he was asleep, but she couldn't wake him up. There was no sign that he'd ever tried using solvents before, and nobody in his family suspected that anything was wrong.

Gemma is 15. She says that, after the funeral, everyone in the family was in shock. Lots of people felt guilty because they thought they could have said or done something to save him. Dan's parents argued all the time after he died and they seemed to blame each other for Dan's death, although Gemma doesn't think it was anyone's fault, just a horrible accident.

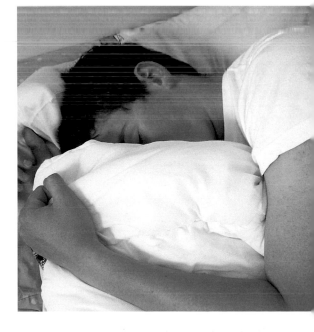

4 Solvent addiction
How and when to get help

If a person is addicted to, or dependent on, something, they feel that they need it in order to get through daily life. They will go to extraordinary lengths to get it, even if doing so has strongly negative effects upon other parts of their life, and they may have unbearable cravings for it. It is possible to become addicted to any substance or activity that affects mood – for example, solvents, alcohol, shopping or video gaming. If someone is addicted to solvents, this means that solvents become the centre of their life, and their relationships and physical and emotional welfare all suffer. People may be more vulnerable to addiction if they have family problems, difficult living conditions or a close relative who is addicted to alcohol or drugs.

Depression
Using solvents to cope with bad feelings can leave you feeling even more stressed and down.

There is psychological and physical addiction. With psychological addiction (also called psychological dependency) alone, the person is often using a substance in an unhealthy way to control highly unpleasant moods, feelings or memories. Physical addiction, or physical dependency, means that when the addicted person stops using a substance they experience unpleasant or even painful sensations (withdrawal symptoms) in their body, in addition to the psychological effects of giving up. Solvents can cause psychological dependency, but are not thought to be physically addictive. Even so, giving up can be very hard, with mood swings, depression and strong cravings.

Unhappy background

A home where there is violence or abuse can make young people more likely to develop an addiction to solvents.

How Janine became addicted

'I started sniffing glue and lighter fuel with friends in my early teens. It seemed like a laugh at the time, and we didn't really think that it was dangerous. I was always the one who did more than everybody else. I had to be completely off my head every time. Some of my friends got scared by the way I was acting, and they probably got sick of having to look after me while I was out of it.

Looking back, I can see that I was feeling very depressed and low and I was using it to get away from my feelings for a while. Things were very bad at home, my step-dad used to get drunk, and he'd get into terrible rages and hit my mum sometimes. We were always afraid he would lash out at one of us, and I thought at the time that there was nobody I could talk to about it. Eventually he moved out, but I still carried on using solvents because I just didn't know how to cope without them.'
(Janine, aged 19)

Signs that you could be developing a problem

Look at the list of signs below. Do any of them apply to you?

- Using solvents, alcohol or other drugs to forget or avoid unpleasant feelings.

- Needing more and more of the substance to get the same effect.

- Thinking about the substance all the time, or having cravings.

- Becoming anxious when you don't have access to the substance, or worrying about where your next supply is coming from.

- Stealing to pay for solvents or other drugs, or stealing the products themselves. Borrowing money from friends or relatives to buy substances.

- Using the substance on an increasingly regular basis.

- Using the substance to stay high continuously for hours throughout the day or evening.

- Becoming aggressive or defensive when people say you're using too much.

- Going off on your own to use the substance, if you normally use it with friends. Becoming more secretive about your use.

- Feeling guilty, empty, hopeless or ashamed after using the substance, or feeling self-hatred.

- Doing things under the influence of intoxication that you regret later.

- Missing work, college or school because of the effects of the substance.

- Wanting to give up, but not feeling able to do so.

- Continuing to abuse the substance even after others have given strong warnings: for example, that you are in danger of losing a job or being thrown out of the house, or that a relationship will be ended.

If you have answered yes to any of these points, you are likely to be at risk of developing a problem. Now would be a good time to cut down, or think about getting some help.

How to find treatment

The best way to start is to make an appointment with your family doctor, but if you don't feel you can do that, you could call one of the helplines on page 62. The doctor and the helplines can refer you to specialist treatment centres and advise about local organizations giving information and support. The doctor can also provide a thorough physical check-up to look for signs of solvent damage, such as problems with nerves or liver and kidney function.

The help available includes one-to-one counselling, family therapy, group therapy, local advice centres and day-care centres. All these treatments aim to help the person develop better coping skills and a healthier lifestyle, while avoiding further solvent abuse.

Confidential help
Your family doctor must treat you in complete confidence and cannot get you into trouble with your family or the police.

One-to-one counselling

Counselling and psychotherapy are 'talking treatments'. The aim of the counsellor or psychotherapist is to help their client to talk about and confront their underlying problems and to resolve them. This also helps to raise the person's self-esteem and boost their confidence. The person is encouraged to recognize and come to terms with the problems that led to them becoming dependent on solvents. These therapies also help people to develop coping mechanisms to make daily life easier to deal with and fill the role that solvents used to play in their lives with something healthier.

'After I'd talked things through with my counsellor, he pointed out that I did more solvents when I was alone and bored. Going to youth clubs twice a week and playing computer games really helped me to cut down.'
(Martin, aged 16)

⊚ Family therapy

Understanding and support from family members can be a huge boost to someone who is trying to give up solvents. It is a stressful time for all concerned, not just the solvent abuser, and parents and other family members can benefit from being able to talk about it with a therapist. If there are hidden problems or tensions in the family that have led to a young person abusing solvents, these can be brought into the open. The therapist can then work with the family to overcome these difficulties.

Group therapy
People in the group can give one another support and share success stories.

⊚ Group therapy

This gives young people a chance to explore the way they think about each other, and their relationships with the outside world. They can share their experiences with other adolescents, learn how to cope with peer pressure and give one another moral support. It can be helpful to an individual to know that they are not alone and isolated with their problems.

Day-care centres (outpatient therapy)

These centres offer an intensive programme of counselling, therapy, group work and education. People attend during the day, rather than staying overnight, and the programmes vary in length depending on how often each person is able to attend.

Local advice centres

Many areas have specialist local centres that help people with dependency problems, and sometimes there are specific solvent abuse centres or programmes. These groups may provide information to children, teenagers and adults, counselling, stress management, art or drama therapy, and many different leisure activities.

Danny's parents are there for him

Danny is 17. His parents found so many empty aerosol cans under his bed that he couldn't get away with yet another cover story. He says his mother freaked out and started crying, which made him feel really scummy and guilty, but at least she didn't shout at him and throw him out of the house. When they got over the shock they had a long talk, and they went with him to see their family doctor, which wasn't nearly as bad as Danny thought it would be. The doctor put him in touch with a local support group who help solvent users, and Danny's parents have even taken days off work to take him there and talk to the people who run it themselves. It really helps Danny to know that his parents are there for him, and they've handled things much better than he expected.

Matt's rescue

'I finally had to admit I'd got a problem when I was fired for missing too many days at work. I went home and had a big binge to take my mind off it, and then the next day I woke up feeling so bad I didn't know what to do. At least the job meant that I couldn't sniff for several hours every day, but now I hardly had a reason to get out of bed. Some of my friends had said they were getting worried about me and one of them got me some leaflets about solvents and what they do to you. I was angry at the time because I thought they were interfering in my life, but I did read the leaflets after they'd gone.

There was a number on one of them for a charity that puts you in touch with treatment centres and support groups in your local area. I picked the phone up four times and put it down again, I was so scared to ring them. It was like making everything real, rather than hoping it would all just go away. When I finally found the nerve to speak to them they were friendly and helpful, and didn't tell me off as if I was stupid or judge me. They just treated me like a normal human being.

I started to go to one-to-one counselling sessions every week, where we talked about the inhalants I was using, why I thought I was doing so much, my family background, that kind of thing. It took a while for me to trust my counsellor. It was the first time in my life that I felt able to talk about my feelings without being scared of being laughed at or put down. That helped me to sort things out better in my own head, and it helped me to stand up for myself more too. I went to a few group therapy sessions and it was good to know that I wasn't alone with my problems.'

Getting through

It takes courage to make the first contact with a support organization, but someone is there, ready for calls like yours.

Staying occupied

Keeping busy and spending time with friends can help to keep your mind off solvents.

Practical ways to help yourself
Planning ahead

Get a support network together, such as mates, parents and your doctor or counsellor. It's much easier than coping alone. Spend time with positive people, and plan a few activities that are enjoyable so that you have things to look forward to. Pick a good time to give up. Try not to make it during a stressful period in your life, when the extra pressure might be too much to cope with, but don't use stress as an excuse to put off stopping! Expect to feel tired and depressed for the first few days, but also expect it to get easier with time. If you have cravings, keep busy and try to keep your mind off them, because they will come and go. Watch a video, call a friend for a chat, or go out for a walk. If you do fail the first time around though, don't beat yourself up, just keep trying.

Many people say that certain situations trigger their addictive behaviour. For example, someone who wants to give up cigarettes may say that being around other smokers, or drinking alcohol, weakens their resolve and makes them more likely to smoke. The first few days and weeks after giving up solvents are usually the most difficult, so it makes sense to avoid the people, places and situations that will be most tempting. It can really help to avoid friends who use solvents, shops where you might buy solvents, or places that you used to go to for the purpose of inhaling. If you are most tempted to use solvents when you are

'When I was giving up, my best friend said I could call her mobile any time, day or night. When the cravings were really bad, it was so good to have someone to talk to.'
(Bev, aged 19)

alone, arrange to be with other people, whether that's trusted friends, relatives or even an evening group where people talk about their addictions.

It may be very difficult to get rid of all the solvents in your home because they are so common in everyday life. Throw out containers of anything you regularly inhale, and wherever possible, buy products with different formulations that do not have the same potential for abuse. For example, buy safety matches instead of lighter fuel, or roll-on or stick deodorants instead of aerosol ones.

Better ways to cope with unpleasant feelings

Don't bottle it all up or try to blot it out with drink or drugs. That only makes things worse in the long run. Find someone to talk to whom you trust. It could be a close friend, a parent or other relative, a teacher, or the school nurse. Begin to express yourself by talking, or writing it all down. Some people say music or art helps them. And don't be ashamed to cry if you're really upset. Be kind to yourself, and treat yourself well if you're having a hard time.

Often, solving your underlying problems can take away the need to abuse solvents. For example, if you abuse solvents because you are bored, then plan some better activities to keep yourself busy. Try to tackle problems instead of avoiding them, and don't be afraid to ask for help if you

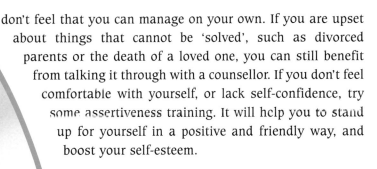

don't feel that you can manage on your own. If you are upset about things that cannot be 'solved', such as divorced parents or the death of a loved one, you can still benefit from talking it through with a counsellor. If you don't feel comfortable with yourself, or lack self-confidence, try some assertiveness training. It will help you to stand up for yourself in a positive and friendly way, and boost your self-esteem.

Looking for excitement and avoiding boredom

If you are looking for something exciting, it doesn't have to be anything that's bad for you. There are other choices. Thrill seekers can go for big amusement park rides, watch scary movies, or try extreme sports, for example. For new experiences, get out and try travelling, learning a language, taking acting lessons, or anything else that interests you. It doesn't have to be like anything you would do at school. If you're bored and miserable, don't sit around at home. Make the effort to find out what's available for young people in your area, such as youth clubs, activity weekends, volunteering or sports clubs.

'I used to get bored
and mope. Mum and dad were
breaking up and had no time for me.
When I finally gave up the glue I joined a band
and discovered I could sing! It made my life
worthwhile, and I never want to go
back to those awful times.'
(Trish, aged 17)

Rollercoaster ride

If you are a thrill seeker, it's fun to share the excitement of the rides at an amusement park.

5 Friends and family
Looking out for others

Signs that someone you know may be using solvents

There are several signs that suggest that someone may be using solvents. However, some of the behaviour in the list below is also common teenage behaviour from time to time, so be careful not to jump to conclusions too quickly.

- Clothes or breath smelling of chemicals.

- Behaving in a 'drunken' or intoxicated manner, but the effects not lasting very long.

- Long-lasting headaches, sore throat, sore eyes or runny nose that have no other explanation.

- With a few brands of glue, there may be a 'sniffer's rash' of spots around the nose and mouth. This is not a feature of all kinds of solvent abuse, and can be confused with acne.

- Sudden changes in behaviour or switching to a new group of friends.

Keep talking
Don't be scared to talk to a friend if you are worried about them.

- Mood swings, and performing less well at school.

- Empty cans of gases, glues or aerosols or used plastic bags lying around where the person has been.

- Loss of appetite, or changes in sleeping habits.

- Clothing with splashes of glue on it.

- Asking for money without saying what it's for, or stealing money from parents.

'It took a long time to convince myself that Jordan was sniffing solvents. The signs were all there, I just couldn't believe he was doing it. When I finally mentioned it to him, the look in his eyes confirmed my worst fears.'
(Anita, aged 45)

Signs that they may be addicted

If someone has become dependent on solvents, they may be using them every day or be using much greater amounts than they did before. They may try to downplay the problem by lying about the real amount they are using or by saying that what they're doing is harmless. They might not be honest about the full extent of the negative effects of their solvent abuse, such as illness, injuries or damage to personal relationships. Their social circle may become one where all their friends are misusing volatile substances, or they may become increasingly isolated as old friends start to avoid them. People who are addicted to any substance are often using it to forget problems or cope with stress. They may also appear to have low self-esteem and are turning to solvents to feel temporarily better about themselves.

Encouraging a friend to seek help

It can be a great help to a volatile substance abuser to know that their friends are supporting them while they try to stop using the solvents. If they want to give up, but don't know where to start, you could find out some more information for them. You could look in the local phone book or library for nearby organizations that help solvent abusers, or you could pick up some booklets or leaflets about solvent abuse. In the UK, there is an organization called Re-Solv which runs a helpline for solvent abusers, their friends and families. The number is at the back of this book.

Try to avoid doing things that will allow your friend to carry on abusing solvents. Don't lend them money to buy more, be persuaded to buy solvents for them, or cover for them when the extent of their abuse makes their life difficult. It might make them feel better in the short term, but in reality it is just making it harder for them to confront their problems. No matter how much you want them to give up, remember that it is their responsibility to give up, not yours. If they don't want to stop abusing solvents, then sadly you will have to accept that there is no way you can force them to do so.

Saying no
It's often hard to say 'no' to a friend who wants to borrow money, but sometimes it is for their own good.

What parents can do

Parents should try not to start an argument if they find their son or daughter has been abusing volatile substances, especially if he or she is still under the influence of the solvents. Anything that is stressful or raises the heart rate can be fatal in this situation. When the young person is not intoxicated, parents can explain their opinion of volatile substance misuse calmly and openly, and point out the dangers. Adults can make sure that teenagers know there is no safe way to abuse solvents and they can kill on the first use.

It's important that parents find out as much about solvent abuse as they can. Teenagers are likely to respect their views more if they have the facts and are not making sensationalist remarks. Forcing an opinion on a teenager can make them rebellious or resentful, so adults should try to have a calm talk with them. They should also listen carefully, for they may discover that their child has personal problems and needs to be encouraged to talk about them. Parents can also take their child to see their GP for a health check and more advice.

If you think that your friend is in serious danger and they won't listen to you, you may have to make the difficult decision to tell a trusted adult. You may worry that your friend will reject you for this, but sometimes it's the right thing to do. Make sure that you look after yourself properly too. Talk to someone if it is stressful, and make sure you make time for yourself to have fun and relax.

Calling for help
Calling an ambulance straight away can save someone's life.

What to do if you find someone intoxicated

If you find someone in an intoxicated state, they could be under the influence of alcohol, street drugs, solvents or a mixture of all of these.

- Although it is a frightening situation, do not panic, shout at the person, shake them, chase them, or start an argument. These things increase the chances of sudden sniffing death.
- If the person is half asleep or appears drunken, keep them awake. DO NOT put them to bed because they might choke on their own vomit while they are unconscious or asleep.
- Gently try to stop them sniffing if they are still inhaling solvents, but do not get into a fight over it.
- Make sure there is plenty of fresh air, and move them gently away from areas with poor ventilation.
- DO NOT give them coffee to rouse them. This may speed up the effects of whatever is in their system.
- If they are anxious or agitated, speak softly and show them how to breathe slowly. Tell them gently that you will look after them until they are feeling better, to help reassure them.
- You may want to call an ambulance or doctor to be on the safe side. Collect up anything that appears to be connected to the incident and show it to the doctor or paramedics. This could be pills, powders, lighter fuel cans, glue, syringes or other suspicious items.

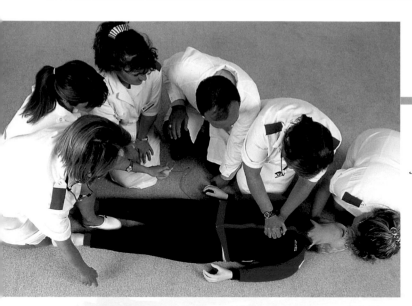

Learning first aid
You can learn CPR on a short first aid course and find out how to keep calm and cope with emergencies.

What to do if you find someone unconscious

- Call out for help and get someone to telephone for an ambulance immediately.
- Gently try to wake the person, but do not shake them hard. Do not slap them, shout in their ear or splash cold water on them to wake them up. This may over-stimulate them if they have been using solvents. These safety measures reduce the risk of sudden sniffing death.
- Check that they are still breathing by looking at the rise and fall of their chest or listening to the area around the nose and mouth. If they are not breathing, be prepared to do CPR (mouth-to-mouth resuscitation) if you have first aid training.
- If they remain unconscious but are still breathing, check their mouth for obstructions such as vomit, quickly scooping obstructions out with your fingers. Loosen any of their clothing that's too tight, to allow them to breathe more easily. Make sure the area is well-ventilated: open doors and windows to allow fresh air into the room.
- Turn them on their side and put them into the recovery position (see page 37). In this position, if they vomit there is less risk of them choking on it.
- If possible, make sure they are not left alone. Check from time to time that they are still breathing.
- Collect up anything that appears to be connected to the incident and show it to the ambulance team. This could be pills, powders, lighter fuel cans, glue, syringes or other suspicious items.

My brother could have died

Zoe found her brother Jack unconscious in his bedroom. He hadn't come downstairs for his evening meal, so Zoe went up to let him know it was ready. He was lying face down on the floor beside the bed, as if he was asleep. There was a strong smell of aerosols in the room and Zoe immediately assumed the worst. She tried to wake him up but nothing worked and she called down to her Dad in a panic. He was quite calm, even though they were both scared, and he made sure that Jack was still breathing.

He got Zoe to open all the doors and windows wide, while he put Jack in the recovery position. Zoe had to wait with Jack while her Dad went downstairs to call an ambulance. She was terrified that he would die while her Dad was out of the room because she didn't really know what to do. Jack was conscious again by the time the paramedics arrived, but they told everyone it was better to be safe than sorry, and that their Dad had done the right thing by calling for help. They checked Jack out and said that he didn't need to go to hospital, but he was lucky not to be injured or even dead.

Jack knows he had a narrow escape, even though he cannot remember much about what happened. He says he was messing around and had no idea of the risks he was taking. The whole family have decided to find out more about solvents and take more time to talk to each other about drugs and other issues.

Glossary

addiction   a state of emotional or physical dependence on a substance or behaviour to get through everyday life, and feeling unable to give it up.

adolescence   the period in human development that lies between the start of puberty and the beginning of adulthood, most commonly in the teenage years.

aerosol   a substance, such as paint or insecticide, dispensed from a small container or canister under pressure, using a propellant. This makes a mist or fog which contains tiny liquid or solid particles.

arrhythmia   any variation from the normal heartbeat. If severe enough this can be fatal, because the heart is beating inefficiently and the body's tissues become damaged due to lack of oxygen.

asphyxiation   restricted breathing, or suffocation. This causes a lack of oxygen in the blood, and if severe and prolonged it can cause death.

butane   commonly abused fuel gas, found in lighter fuel refills. It is the substance linked to the largest number of volatile substance abuse deaths.

carcinogenic   having the potential to cause cancer.

cardiac arrest   the sudden stopping of the heart.

CPR   abbreviation of 'cardio-pulmonary resuscitation'. This first-aid technique may save the life of a person who is not breathing and whose heart has stopped beating.

cold injuries   damage caused to human tissues when they are exposed to very low temperatures. This includes frostbite and tissue swelling. The injuries can be caused by gases escaping from pressurized canisters.

cravings   unpleasant and intense desires or longing for a substance, especially felt when someone is addicted to it and is trying to give it up.

dependency   psychological or physical reliance on a substance such as solvents or street drugs, usually with strong cravings.

depressant   a substance that is capable of diminishing or reducing nervous activity. Solvents and alcohol affect brain function in this way.

disinhibition   a condition where the behaviour or mental state of a person is less restrained than usual.

encephalitis   an inflammation of the brain, causing pain, unconsciousness or sometimes death. People who recover from encephalitis may be left with permanent brain damage.

experimental use   where something is tried only once or twice out of curiosity.

flammable   liable to catch fire extremely easily. 'Inflammable' has the same meaning.

hallucination   the false perception of an object that is not truly present. Most hallucinations associated with solvents are visual.

hydrocarbons   small compounds made up of carbon and hydrogen atoms.

inhalants   volatile substances that are deliberately breathed in to cause intoxication.

inhale   take in deep breaths of vapour through the mouth or nose.

intoxication — a state ranging from euphoria to stupor, usually accompanied by loss of inhibitions and control.

myocardium — the muscular tissues of the heart. They can become over-sensitized to the effects of the stress hormone adrenaline (epinephrine) after someone inhales volatile substances.

nausea — the sensations that occur before someone vomits; 'feeling sick'.

peer pressure — pressure to behave in the same way as the other people in the same social group, such as classmates or friends. There is often a fear of being unpopular or abandoned by friends.

propellant — the gas that is used to carry the liquid droplets or solid particles in an aerosol spray.

recreational use — where a substance is used from time to time, usually as part of a social group of friends. Recreational use of solvents generally lasts for a few weeks or months only.

self-esteem — a feeling of self-respect and liking yourself, feeling good about yourself.

sniffing — in the context of solvent abuse, inhaling vapours deeply through the nose and mouth to become intoxicated.

solvent — strictly speaking, any substance that can be used to dissolve another, for example water. The solvents in this book are all volatile substances that can be abused.

solvent abuse — deliberately inhaling the vapours from solvents and volatile substances for the purpose of becoming intoxicated.

sudden sniffing death — death caused when the heart or lungs quickly cease to function, causing a fatal lack of oxygen to the body's tissues. It is responsible for about half of all solvent-related deaths.

suffocation — the deprivation of oxygen, caused by blockage of the airways, covering mouth and nose with large plastic bags, or inhalation of gases.

tolerance — state of needing more and more of a substance to get the same effects, especially after using the substance heavily for a long time.

toluene — a volatile flammable liquid, obtained from petroleum and coal tar, which is found in many glues.

toxic — poisonous.

vagus nerve — a large nerve that runs from the base of the brain to the heart, lungs and abdomen. It can be affected by spraying solvents directly into the mouth, thus slowing or stopping the heartbeat.

vapours — particles of liquid that are suspended in the air; fumes or gases given off by liquid solvents.

ventilation — a supply of fresh air that drives fumes away. This can be as simple as opening a window to allow solvent gases to escape, or as complex as an industrial air conditioning system.

volatile substances — chemicals that can readily change form from a liquid or a solid into a vapour. In volatile substance abuse, the chemicals used all have effects upon a person's state of mind and are mostly hydrocarbons.

Resources

Re-Solv

The Society for the Prevention of Solvent and Volatile Substance Abuse, or Re-Solv, is a national charity solely dedicated to the prevention of solvent and volatile substance abuse (VSA). Their helpline operators have access to a UK-wide databank of referral agencies to enable them to refer callers to facilities in their area. They also provide factsheets for teenagers and parents, and educational materials for schools.

Telephone: 0808 800 2345 Monday-Friday, 9am-5pm (excluding public holidays)

www.re-solv.org

National Drugs Helpline

This organization offers free and confidential advice about any drugs issue, including solvents, whether callers are looking for information, counselling or just a chat. They can also give callers information about services in their local area. Lines are open 24 hours a day.

Telephone: 0800 77 66 00
www.ndh.org.uk

DrugScope

This is a leading UK drugs charity and centre of expertise on drugs. It aims to provide balanced and up-to-date drug information to professionals and the public. It has an excellent library and there is specific solvents and volatile substances information on the website.

Telephone: 020 7928 1211
www.drugscope.org.uk

NHS Direct

This service provides information about solvent misuse as part of an online self-help information section. Includes statistics, dangers, and help for users and parents.

Telephone: 0845 46 47 (open 24 hours a day)
www.nhsdirect.nhs.uk

St George's Hospital Medical School

The Public Health Sciences department has been maintaining a register of all UK deaths from volatile substance abuse for about 20 years. It produces an annual report, supported by the Department of Health, which is distributed to anyone interested.

Disclaimer

The website addresses (URLs) included in this book were valid at the time of going to press. However, because of the nature of the internet, it is possible that some addresses may have changed, or sites may have changed or closed down since publication. While the author and the publishers regret any inconvenience this may cause readers, no responsibility for any such changes can be accepted by either the author or the publishers.

Index

SOLVENTS